RESOLVING CONFLICTS JUST LIKE JESUS CHRIST

DR MIRIAM KINAI

ISBN: 1477567186

ISBN-13: 978-1477567180

CONTENTS

A

THE FIRST CONFLICT

CONFLICT COMPLEXITIES

THE FIRST CONFLICT

JESUS,

THE PHARISEES &

THE ADULTEROUS WOMAN

Now early in the morning He came again into the temple, and all the people came to Him; and He sat down and taught them.

Then the scribes and Pharisees brought to Him a woman caught in adultery.

And when they had set her in the midst, they said to Him, "Teacher, this woman was caught in adultery, in the very act.

Now Moses, in the law, commanded us that such should be stoned. But what do You say?"

This they said, testing Him, that they might have something of which to accuse Him.

But Jesus stooped down and wrote on the ground with His finger, as though He did not hear.

So when they continued asking Him, He raised Himself up and said to them,

"He who is without sin among you, let him throw a stone at her first."

And again He stooped down and wrote on the ground.

Then those who heard it, being convicted by their

conscience, went out one by one, beginning with the oldest even to the last.

And Jesus was left alone, and the woman standing in the midst.

When Jesus had raised Himself up and saw no one but the woman, He said to her, "Woman, where are those accusers of yours? Has no one condemned you?"

She said, "No one, Lord."

And Jesus said to her, "Neither do I condemn you; go and sin no more." (John 8:2-11)

CONFLICT COMPLEXITIES

Mediating Conflictor

Tight Lipped Conflictor

Uneven Balance Of Power

Poor Positioning

Inappropriate Place

Inopportune Time

Mob Psychology

Intellectual Intimidation

Moral Condescension

Gender Insensitivity

Cultural Biases

Ulterior Motives

It is crucial for you to note the 12 complexities in this conflict so that you can learn to recognize them in the conflicts you may be embroiled in or in those you may be called upon to mediate.

Identifying these potential mines and learning how Jesus navigated His way around them will help you steer your home, ministry or business safely around them as you resolve conflicts more effectively.

I

MEDIATING CONFLICTOR

The first party in this conflict was the group of Pharisees and scribes. The second party was the woman since she was caught contravening the Law of Moses that the Pharisees and scribes advocated and enforced.

Jesus became the third party when they brought the conflict to Him and asked for His opinion for **They said to Him, "Teacher, this woman was caught in adultery, in the very act. Now Moses, in the law, commanded us that such should be stoned. But what do you say?"**

His was therefore not strictly mediating between the woman and the Pharisees for the latter suspected that He would say something different from the Law of Moses and that is why they were **Testing Him, that they might have something of which to accuse Him.**

Learn from Jesus for though He was in a tricky situation, He was able to stand up for His teachings on mercy and save the woman's life without breaking the Law of Moses that the scribes prescribed.

With just one sentence, He therefore resolved the conflict by successfully marrying the law to love and custom with compassion. So, learn to assert yourself without upsetting others.

II

TIGHT-LIPPED CONFLICTOR

Talking is very important in conflict resolution but in some instances one of the conflicting parties may choose to remain silent for a number of reasons.

This woman's unadulterated shame or the shock or guilt of being **Caught in adultery, in the very act** and then dragged to the Temple could have silenced her.

Being accused by multiple powerful Pharisees could have also intimidated her into speechlessness.

In other conflicts, anger can make one of the parties refrain from speaking. They may also sulk in an attempt to punish the other party for hurting their feelings.

Frustration can also make them mute if they think their needs won't be met whether they verbalize them or not.

Note that even if one party does not say a word, they still talk nonverbally. When **Jesus stooped down and wrote on the ground with His finger, as though He did not hear,** He could have been listening to what the woman was saying without words.

So study their each party's body language for silent clues to their thoughts and feelings.

III

UNEVEN BALANCE OF POWER

The balance of human power was leaning strongly in favor of the Pharisees and scribes as these were influential men held in high regard by the community.

Jesus also had some authority, for a crowd had already gathered to listen to His teaching and even the Pharisees addressed Him respectfully as **"Teacher"**.

The woman on the other hand, had been rendered powerless and worthy only of death by virtue of her unvirtuous crime for she had been **Caught in adultery, in the very act!**

She was not even addressed by her name for the Pharisees referred to her as **"This woman"** and later as **"Such"** when they said, **"Such should be stoned"**.

When in a similar situation, do not let yourself be manipulated either overtly or covertly by the parties that are stronger numerically, monetarily or politically.

Moreover, sidestep succumbing to reverse discrimination whereby the top dogs are discriminated against just because they are strong in favor of the underdogs. Be fair to all the parties just like Jesus.

IV

POOR POSITIONING

The positioning of the parties was also not appropriate for effective conflict resolution for the Pharisees brought the woman and **Set her in the midst** of a crowd.

She was placed in the middle of her many accusers and **All the people** Jesus had been teaching. This was a nerve-racking arrangement as countless censuring eyes converged on her from all corners and it may have been one reason why she couldn't speak up for herself.

It would have been better if she had been told to stand on one side, facing her accusers, rather than in the middle of a mob of men baying for her blood.

If you are unable to influence the sitting (or standing arrangement) as Jesus may have been, do what you can to make all parties feel comfortable.

You can bend down to a child's eye level for when **Jesus stooped down and wrote on the ground with His finger,** He could have assumed this position to get down to her level so that He would not be towering over her like the others.

V

INAPPROPRIATE PLACE

By bringing the conflict to the Temple, a sacred place of worship, the Pharisees complicated it for that was not the ideal place for disagreeing parties to meet let alone to discuss an issue like adultery.

It was also the Pharisee's turf and they were likely to be joined by like minded peers while it was highly unlikely that anyone would dare side with a woman accused of such an immoral crime in such a sacrosanct place.

By bringing the woman there, the Pharisees were also putting her on public display for her private crime for it was a public place and people had already gathered to listen to Jesus' teaching. It therefore lacked the privacy to solve any crisis let alone a personal one.

If, like in Jesus' case, you are unable to influence the choice of venue, make the best use of where you are like He did.

If you can, choose a place not owned any of the conflicting parties and not where any of their supporters normally congregate.

VI

INOPPORTUNE TIME

The timing also complicated the conflict for Jesus was already teaching when the Pharisees brought the woman. It does not seem that they had notified Him in advance that they'd bring a conflict for Him to resolve at that particular time.

But, Jesus stopped teaching and begun resolving the conflict even though it may have inconvenienced His day's schedule.

He even took His time for after listening, **Jesus stooped down and wrote on the ground with His finger.** He could have done this to buy time to think or pray for a solution but in any case, He did not rush through the process.

Therefore, if you find yourself entangled in a grave conflict, take time off from your tight schedule and resolve it at once. Take as much time as you need, just like Jesus did, to ensure a satisfactory conclusion. He did not rush the process so that He could get back to preaching.

So do not dash through the resolution process however inconveniencing it maybe. Don't rush it even if it is another party which has the most at stake for in His case, it was the woman who was threatened with the grave and not Jesus.

11

VII

MOB PSYCHOLOGY

The Pharisees and scribes came as a group and joined **All the people** who were already being taught by Jesus.

After they presented their case, **Jesus stooped down and wrote on the ground.** He may have done this to retreat into Himself and create mental space between Him and the mob so that He could make a decision not influenced by their urgency or expectations.

Therefore, when facing a mob, mentally withdraw from it's pandemonium so that you can make an independent decision.

Don't let their numbers, noise or physical presence pressurize you. Make the same decision you would have made if there was just one Pharisee and one woman.

In addition, choose your words carefully like Jesus, for a mob confers a sense of protective anonymity to its individual members and this seems to give them the license to perform illegal, immoral or inhuman acts as they feel they won't be singled out for the group's terrible acts. So, do not aggravate or agitate it further.

As a mob can evolve into a dangerous force with the members feeding on each other's energy, use silence as a weapon to counter it's racket like Jesus did when He **Stooped down and wrote on the ground ... as though he did not hear.**

VIII

INTELLECTUAL INTIMIDATION

The Pharisees and scribes who were the interpreters and teachers of the Law of Moses said to Jesus, "**Now Moses, in the law, commanded us that such should be stoned. But what do you say?**"

By adding the "**But**" before the "**What do you say?**", they were implying that He'd have a different opinion from theirs and Moses'. In essence, they were saying, "We, learned Law of Moses Specialists, submit that this woman should be stoned according to the Law of Moses. But what do you, a carpenter's Son have to say?"

Emulate Jesus, who knew the Law of Moses, and don't be intimidated by specialists if you have a decent grasp of the subject even if they quote specialized texts, journals and websites in an attempt to prove their undisputable authority in that topic and to coerce you to submissively accept their suggestions.

Even if they say that they have the only correct analysis of the facts due to the fact that they are experts and suggest that you aren't qualified or experienced enough to challenge them, if your information is accurate and up-to-date, hold your ground with it.

If you don't understand the facts, ask for clarification or hire a neutral consultant in that field to help you.

Conversely, if you know more about any of the issues than the other parties, do not blatantly bring it to their attention.

Jesus did not brag about His universal knowledge. He simply said what He had to say and the Pharisees recognized His deep wisdom. The older ones, who were the first ones to leave, appreciating it faster than the younger ones.

So, let your words of wisdom speak for themselves and the other parties will recognize your authority in that area for **Who is wise and understanding among you? Let him show by good conduct that his works are done in the meekness of wisdom.** (James 3:13)

IX

MORAL CONDESCENSION

The Pharisees referred to the woman as **"Such"**, to demean her and present themselves as morally superior in order influence the conflict resolution process.

Copy Jesus who sensed their tactlessness and tactfully worked a solution around it by giving His opinion without looking down on any of the parties.

Though He Himself had never sinned, He didn't judge the supercilious scribes and Pharisees though He knew they were sinners for He said, **"He who is without sin among you, let him throw a stone at her first"** and they all left without throwing a single stone for they were all **Convicted by their conscience.**

He also didn't denounce the lady for He **Said to her, "Neither do I condemn you".**

So, treat everyone with dignity and don't be swayed by people's pretentiousness. Don't look down on anyone regardless of how tarnished their reputations are.

Don't also give undue credence to those who infer with their looks, words or deeds that since they stand on the morally high ground their words carry more weight than those of the parties said to be groveling in the gutters of depravity.

X

GENDER INSENSITIVITY

The Pharisees came with the woman and **Set her in the midst** of the multitude.

They placed her in the middle of very many men for the Pharisees and scribes were all men and the crowd that was being taught by Jesus probably constituted only of men for He said to them, **"He who is without sin among you, let him throw a stone at her first."**

By placing the lone woman in the midst of a male mob while accusing her of committing a crime with a man who was not facing the same death sentence, the male Pharisees demonstrated grand gender insensitivity.

Imitate Jesus, a man, who handled the delicate issue with sensitivity. He didn't bring any undue attention to her even when she did not speak up for herself.

In fact, He may have even bent down to write on the ground to shift the focus of those gawking male eyes from her to what He was writing on the ground.

His words also diverted their attention from her immoral deed to their inner selves and personal sins for after He had spoken, **Those who heard it** were **Convicted by their conscience.**

XI

CULTURAL BIASES

While the Pharisees and scribes adhered to Moses' Law, it is not clear if this woman was of the same belief system.

If you are embroiled in a dispute with people with different beliefs or entangled in an intercultural conflict, do not use words that may be construed as insulting or describe any party's beliefs or customs as barbaric, outdated or superstitious.

Keep your opinions about their cultural practices to yourself so that you can amicably arrive at a cross-culturally acceptable solution.

If asked for your personal opinion, champion Christ-like behavior, Christian principles and common sense which cut across cultures and all parties should be **Convicted by their conscience.**

XII

ULTERIOR MOTIVES

The Pharisees brought the woman to Jesus not because they cared so much about the state of marriages or her lifestyle choices but mainly because they wanted to test Jesus **That they might have something of which to accuse Him.**

After they had presented their case, **Jesus stooped down and wrote on the ground with His finger, as though He did not hear.** He could have done this to pray silently while writing. So, before you speak, pray for discernment to determine if there is more than what is been said.

In addition learn to listen carefully for the Pharisees words may have given them away for they said, **"Now Moses, in the law, commanded us that such should be stoned. But what do You say?"** By phrasing their question this way, they were challenging Jesus to see if He would dare contradict the Law of Moses.

Look also, at the circumstances surrounding the conflict. The Pharisees came to Jesus after **All the people came to Him; and He sat down and taught them.** They may have done this to discredit Him by proving to His students that His teachings were contrary to the Law and also to ensure that His many students would later be their many witnesses.

B

THE SECOND CONFLICT

CONFLICT RESOLUTION STRATEGIES

THE SECOND CONFLICT

DAVID,

NABAL & ABIGAIL

There was a man in Maon ... and the man was very rich. He had 3000 sheep and a 1000 goats ... The name of the man was Nabal, and the name of his wife Abigail. And she was a woman of good understanding and beautiful appearance; but the man was harsh and evil in his doings ...

David sent 10 young men ... "Go to Nabal ... say to him ... 'Your shepherds were with us, and we did not hurt them, nor was there anything missing from them ... Ask your young men, and they will tell you. Therefore let my young men find favor in your eyes, for we come on a feast day. Please give whatever comes to your hand to your servants and to your son David.' "

So when David's young men came, they spoke to Nabal ... Nabal answered ... and said, "Who is David, and who is the son of Jesse? ... Shall I then take my bread and my water and my meat ... and give it to men when I do not know where they are from?"

So David's young men ... went back ... told him ... Then David said ... "Every man gird on his sword." So every man girded on his sword, and David also girded on his sword... about 400 men...

One of the young men told Abigail ... "Look, David sent messengers ... to greet your master;

and he reviled them. But the men were very good to us, and we were not hurt, nor did we miss anything as long as we accompanied them ...

Now therefore, know and consider what you will do, for harm is determined against our master and against all his household. For he is such a scoundrel that one cannot speak to him."

Then Abigail made haste and took 200 loaves of bread, 2 skins of wine, 5 sheep already dressed, 5 seahs of roasted grain, 100 clusters of raisins, and 200 cakes of figs, and loaded them on donkeys ... But she did not tell her husband Nabal.

So it was, as she rode on the donkey ... there were David and his men, coming down toward her, and she met them.

Now David had said, "Surely in vain I ... protected all that this fellow has ... And he has repaid me evil for good." ...

When Abigail saw David, she dismounted quickly from the donkey, fell on her face before David, and bowed down... She... said: "On me, my lord, on me let this iniquity be!... Please, let not my lord regard this scoundrel Nabal. For as his name is, so is he: Nabal is his name, and folly is with him! ...

I ...did not see the young men ... you sent ... And now this present which your maidservant has brought ... let it be given to the young men who follow my lord.

Please forgive the trespass of your maidservant.

For the Lord will ... make for my lord an enduring house, because ... evil is not found in you throughout your days. Yet a man has risen to pursue you and seek your life, but the life of my lord shall be bound in the bundle of the living with the Lord your God; and the lives of your enemies He shall sling out, as from the pocket of a sling.

And it shall come to pass, when the Lord has ... appointed you ruler over Israel, that this will be of no grief to you, nor offense of heart to my lord, either that you have shed blood without cause, or that my lord has avenged himself ...

Then David said to Abigail: "Blessed is the Lord God of Israel ... And blessed is your advice ... because you have kept me this day from coming to bloodshed and from avenging myself with my own hand. For indeed ... unless you had hurried and come to meet me, surely by morning light no males would have been left to Nabal!"

So David received from her hand what she had brought him, and said to her, "Go up in peace to your house. See, I have heeded your voice and respected your person."

Now Abigail went to Nabal, and there he was, holding a feast ... he was very drunk; therefore she told him nothing ...

In the morning, when the wine had gone from Nabal, and his wife had told him ... his heart died within him, and he became like stone. Then ... after about 10 days ... the Lord stuck Nabal, and he died. (1 Samuel 25:2-38)

CONFLICT RESOLUTION STRATEGIES

Pray Over It

Prepare For It

Pay Attention

Picture It

Ponder Over It

Put It In Words

Proffer Something

Procure Something

Pass Over Pitfalls

Pick A Solution

Pass Through Impasses

Put It In Writing

I

PRAY OVER IT

Talk to God before talking to the other parties and learn to **Lean not on your own understanding; in all your ways acknowledge Him, and He shall direct your paths.** (Proverbs 3:5-6)

Ask Him to guide you along the conflict resolution path and then hasten upon it.

Learn from Abigail that time is of great essence when resolving conflicts for after learning of the one between David and her husband, **Abigail made haste ... As she rode on the donkey ... there were David and his men, coming down toward her.** They were **about 400 men**, all armed.

She did not postpone her journey and thus she was able to save her family and business for when she met David, he said to her, **"Unless you had hurried and come to meet me, surely by morning light no males would have been left to Nabal!"**

Therefore, **Go and humble yourself; plead with your friend. Give no sleep to you eyes, nor slumber to your eyelids. Deliver yourself like a gazelle from the hand of the hunter, and like a bird from the hand of the fowler.** (Proverbs 6:3-5)

Make resolving conflicts a priority for postponing it increases stress as you live in tension dreading the moment you will inevitably have to deal with them.

Delaying resolving conflicts also fosters bitterness

that can condense into hatred and congeal into plans to harm you by those who think you have hurt them.

So set out to settle your conflicts as soon as they arise in order to improve your relationships whether these are spousal, parent-child, siblings, employer-employee, co-workers or neighbors.

If you are not able to settle them at once, settle on the time when you'll sit face to face with the other parties to work it out.

Try to resolve conflicts in person rather than over the phone or via email as this leaves less room for misunderstanding to fester as they can be quickly corrected before they breed new conflicts.

II

PREPARE FOR IT

Preparing will help you resolve your conflicts faster and leave the negotiation table content. To help you decide what you want to achieve from the conflict resolution process write down:

A. All your interests that are threatened by the conflict in order of importance.

B. How you want the conflict to be resolved.

C. What you are willing to concede as you compromise to reach a solution.

D. What you want to retain as you negotiate to reach a solution.

From Abigail, we can learn how to prepare effectively using the above steps:

A. Her interests that were threatened by the conflict between her husband Nabal and David were the lives of all the men in her family and working for her for **David said to Abigail: "… Surely by morning light no males would have been left to Nabal!"**

B. Abigail wanted the conflict to be resolved and the men's lives spared for she said to David, **"That this will be of no grief to you, nor offense of heart to my lord, either that you have shed blood without cause, or that my lord has avenged himself."**

C. In order to compromise and reach a solution, Abigail was willing to "trade off" some things for she **Took 200 loaves of bread, 2 skins of wine, 5 sheep already dressed, 5 seahs of roasted grain, 100 clusters of raisins, and 200 cakes of figs, and loaded them on donkeys.**

D. As she compromised, Abigail wanted to retain the lives of the men of her household and business as evidenced by her words (see **B** above).

Therefore, know and consider what you will do by walking through the above steps before you meet the other parties to resolve your conflict.

III

PAY ATTENTION

After preparing, meet the other parties and listen as they present their case for listening is the key to resolving conflicts.

Listen attentively for **He who answers a matter before he hears it, it is folly and shame to him.** (Proverbs 18:13)

Pay special attention to the issues being emphasized even if you've heard it all before for you might get a new insight into the recurring problem that will finally solve it. In addition to listening to the words being said, you also have to:

LISTEN ACTIVELY

Active listening involves using positive body language such as nodding your head and leaning toward the speaker as you maintain eye contact with them.

It is important because when the other parties see that you are taking their concerns seriously, they are also more likely to take yours seriously.

Don't fidget, yawn, look around the room or glance at your watch as you edgily wait for them to stop talking.

Instead, focus on their facial expressions, eye movements, muscle twitches, hair twirling, fist clenching, arm or leg crossing and other nonverbal cue to assess their sentiments and sincerity.

Take note of the facts and the feelings, the sighs and suggestions. Listen for changes in their inflection as they may tell you which of the verbalized issues touches a sore spot.

In addition, pay attention to the silences linking the sentences and the nuances tinting the nouns as they might hold a clue as to what is not being said but holds the key to resolving the conflict.

IV

PICTURE IT

After listening, ask questions to get a clear picture of the contentious issues so that your response is not based on conjecture.

Seek further clarification by rephrasing their words like King Solomon did after listening to the 2 conflicting women, for **The king said, "The one says, 'This is my son, who lives, and your son is the dead one'; and the other says, 'No! But your son is the dead one, and my son is the living one.'"** (1 Kings 3:23)

You can begin paraphrasing by saying,

"As I understand it, you are saying ..."

Rephrasing their words also helps them see the issue from your perspective and this can help you both reach an agreement. Therefore, don't hesitate to take a few minutes to paraphrase their opinions.

V

PONDER OVER IT

After grasping the issues, think before you respond for **Do you see a man hasty in his words? There is more hope for a fool than for him.** (Proverbs 29:20)

Copy Jesus who wasn't hasty with His words for after the Pharisees had spoken, **Jesus stooped down and wrote on the ground** (John 8:2-11) before He spoke. He may have been pondering His reply so write down your thoughts and analyze them for **The heart of the righteous studies how to answer.** (Proverbs 15:28)

VI

PUT IT IN WORDS

After planning your response, publicize it. To do so effectively, you have to:

SPEAK GENTLY

A soft answer turns away wrath, but a harsh word stirs up anger. (Proverbs 15:1) Abigail proved this for her soft words turned away David's anger which her husband's harsh words had stirred.

She spoke gently and David relented for **A gentle tongue breaks a bone.** (Proverbs 25:15)

So speak gently as you do not have to shout to be heard. It also gives you a slight psychological edge for it gives the impression that you are in control.

Soften harsh facts by communicating calmly, not condescendingly, audibly but not abrasively and the other parties will be more willing to adopt your proposals.

Learn from Abigail and **Let your speech always be with grace, seasoned with salt, that you may know how you ought to answer each one.** (Colossians 4:6) She spoke of David killing Goliath with a sling and King Saul unjustly trying to kill him by saying, **A man has risen to pursue you and seek your life, but the life of my lord shall be bound in the bundle of the living with the Lord your God; and the lives of your enemies He shall sling out, as from the pocket of a sling.**

TAKE RESPONSIBILITY

If your words or actions or omissions contributed to the genesis of the conflict, take responsibility for your contribution.

If you didn't play a part, but you are representing the person who did like Abigail, take responsibility like she did for she said to David, **"On me, my lord, on me let this iniquity be!"**

Do not shift the blame to another party like Adam and Eve did after eating the forbidden fruit when they were asked by God, **"Have you eaten from the tree of which I commanded you that you should not eat?" Then the man said, "The woman whom You gave to be with me, she gave me of the tree, and I ate."**

And the Lord God said to the woman, "What is this you have done?" The woman said, "The serpent deceived me, and I ate." (Genesis 3:11-13)

After taking responsibility for your actions, ask for forgiveness like Abigail for she said to David, **Please forgive the trespass of your maidservant.**

So, accept responsibility, apologize, ask for forgiveness and you will resolve your conflicts faster for **He who covers his sins will not prosper, but whoever confesses and forsakes them will have mercy.** (Proverbs 28:13)

ASSERT YOURSELF

Communicate your response clearly without minimizing what you want to say or hurting the feelings of the other parties.

Focus on the issues that are important to you and ensure everyone understands you.

To assert yourself, remember the mnemonic:

A Assess your problems, feelings, goals

S Set a convenient place to meet

S State the problem clearly

E Express feelings using "I" sentences

R Request for what you want

T Tell them the consequences

At this stage in the conflict resolution process focus on the **E** & **R**.

BE HUMBLE

Assert yourself humbly for **By pride comes nothing but strife.** (Proverbs 13:16)

Emulate wealthy Abigail who displayed great humility for **when Abigail saw David, she dismounted quickly from the donkey, fell on her face before David, and bowed down to the ground.**

So, get off your high horse and even if you don't prostrate yourself physically, you can prostrate yourself verbally by using modest language for **A man's pride will bring him low, but the humble in spirit will retain honor.** (Proverbs 29:23)

VII

PROFFER SOMETHING

After expressing your thoughts and feelings on the contentious issues, encourage a give and take approach whereby all parties give something and take something from each other.

Set the ball rolling by making some concessions. Go through your list of the items that you are willing to cede to the other party to meet their needs so that the conflict can be resolved. Offer them one item or give in to one demand that fills one of their most pressing needs.

Emulate Abigail who said to David, **And now this present which your maidservant has brought to my lord, let it be given to the young men who follow my lord.**

She then gave him **200 loaves of bread, 2 skins of wine, 5 sheep already dressed, 5 seahs of roasted grain, 100 clusters of raisins, and 200 cakes of figs.**

This was what David had wanted when he sent his emissaries to Nabal for he had said, **Let my young men find favor in your eyes, for we come on a feast day. Please give whatever comes to your hand to your servant and to your son David.**

VIII

PROCURE SOMETHING

After proffering, go through your list of threatened interests and ask for one thing that fills your most pressing need.

Abigail did so by asking David to spare the men. She said, **That it will be of no grief to you, nor offense of heart ... either that you have shed blood without cause, or that my lord has avenged himself.**

If the other parties attempt to evade giving in to you one request, assert yourself with carefully worded sentence.

IX

PASS OVER PITFALLS

Heed the following to avoid the pitfalls that can derail resolving a conflict:

THOU SHALL NOT

USE COMMUNICATION BLOCKS

Avoid accusations, arrogance, changing the subject, condemning comments, high-pressure persuasion, insulting language, interrupting speakers, outright lying, quarrelsome tones, rudeness and sarcasm as they are counterproductive to achieving your goal of resolving the conflict.

THOU SHALL NOT

BELITTLE ANYONE

Do not trivialize the other parties' concerns or comments. Do not discredit their characters, logic or morality.

Do not utter statements such as:

"This is a very childish or stupid or time wasting complaint"

"That is a very coldhearted suggestion"

"You must be joking! How can you even think something like that?"

THOU SHALL NOT

USE GENERALIZATIONS

Convey that each party's concerns are unique and valid and avoid using generalities such as:

"You always ..." or

"You never..." or

"You Pharisees are all the same."

THOU SHALL

MANAGE YOUR EMOTIONS

Manage your emotions. Don't let them manage you. Copy Abigail for she didn't let her emotions splinter her thinking or taint her speech from when she knew of her family's impending massacre to when she met David and his army for **She was a woman of good understanding**.

Since **A man of understanding is of a calm spirit** (Proverbs 17:27) try to always remain cool, calm and collected. If irked, take deep breaths to calm down and **Do not hasten in your spirit to be angry, for anger rests in the bosom of fools.** (Ecclesiastes 7:8-9) Then sieve your words with restraint for **A fool vents all his feelings, but a wise man holds them back.** (Proverbs 29:11)

THOU SHALL

MANAGE THEIR EMOTIONS

If there is a hostile response to something you have said, keep quiet instead of fueling the fire with more words. Don't rush to defend or justify yourself as it will only agitate them further. Keep your cool, exercise tolerance and resist the urge to fight or insult back for **The discretion of a man makes him slow to anger, and his glory is to overlook a transgression.** (Proverbs 19:11)

Let some of the abuse, accusations and attacks pass and when you do speak, be polite and **Do not answer a fool according to his folly, lest you also be like him.** (Proverbs 26:4)

If the other parties lose their temper, stop talking for silence may help them cool off. If you feel threatened, excuse yourself and leave the room. Give them time and space to calm down.

Copy Jesus who gave the Pharisees time to calm down when they came baying for the lady's blood as He **stooped down and wrote on the ground.** (John 8:2-11) He spoke after their emotions had settled and they were more likely to hear and heed His words.

So start speaking when they are composed and speak calmly to set the tone at which the talks will continue. Begin by acknowledging their emotions using "I" sentences such as "*I can see you are upset*" which shows them that you have registered their words and actions.

THOU SHALL NOT

MANIPULATE

Jesus didn't let the Pharisees manipulate Him when they came heated because the **woman was caught in adultery.** (John 8:2-11) He made a decision that wasn't influenced by their numbers, power, urgency, fury or self-righteousness.

Copy Him and don't let the other parties words, actions or emotions push you into a solution that isn't in your best interest.

If they gesture aggressively, move away. If they begin to cry, don't drown with self destructive pity in their tears.

In addition, do not manipulate them if you have the upper hand.

X

PICK A SOLUTION

As the aim of conflict resolution is for all the parties to win in some way and not for one party to win at the expense of the others, pick a solution that protects some (if not all) the interests of all the parties.

Emulate Jesus whose solution of, **"He who is without sin among you, let him throw a stone at her first"** (John 8:2-11), protected the interests of all the parties.

He protected His interests which were His teachings on love and mercy. He protected the woman's interests for her life was spared. And, He also protected the Pharisees' interests for He did not break the Law of Moses.

Abigail's solution also protected hers and David's interests for she said, **When the Lord has ... appointed you ruler over Israel ... it will be of no grief to you, nor offense of heart ... either that you have shed blood without cause, or that my lord has avenged himself.** (1 Samuel 25:2-38)

She protected her interests for her men's lives were spared. And, she protected David's interests for he remained innocent of murder and vengeance.

Therefore, as you pick a solution, **Let each of you look out not only for his own interests, but also for the interests of others.** (Philippians 2:4)

XI

PASS THROUGH IMPASSES

If the discussion reaches a deadlock, take a short break. You can use the break to pray for a breakthrough for **If any of you lacks wisdom, let him ask of God, who gives to all liberally and without reproach, and it will be given to him.** (James 1:5)

If there is tension in the air, cut it with a tasteful joke.

Or, you can also sit in silence as each party reflects on the issues for the calm after a stormy debate may clear your minds making the solution crystal clear.

After the break, ask the parties to shift their attention from the problem or impassable area to a possible solution.

Jesus deftly shifted the Pharisees' focus from the problem of the woman's sinful deed to the solution of forgiveness since everyone had sinned for He said, **"He who is without sin among you, let him throw a stone at her first."** (John 8:2-11)

Abigail also shifted David's focus from the problem of Nabal behavior and him avenging himself by killing her men for she said, **Please, let not my lord regard this scoundrel Nabal. For as his name is, so is he: Nabal is his name, and folly is with him!** She turned David's attention to the solution, which was her gift to him and his men.

If you are not able to pass through the impasses and arrive at a solution by yourselves, suggest resolving the conflict with the help of a mediator and switch the discussion to choosing a mediator.

Choose a Christian, if possible, for **Dare any of you, having a matter against another, go to law before the unrighteous, and not before the saints?**

Do you not know that the saints will judge the world? And if the world will be judged by you, are you unworthy to judge the smallest matters? Do you not know that we shall judge angels? How much more, things that pertain to this life?

If then you have judgments concerning things pertaining to this life, do you appoint those who are least esteemed by the church to judge? (1 Corinthians 6:1-7)

In addition, choose a mediator with more experience in the contentious issues. Learn from King Rehoboam's mistake when the Israelites said to him, **"Your father made our yoke heavy; now therefore, lighten the burdensome service of your father, and his heavy yoke which he put on us, and we will serve you."** ...

King Rehoboam consulted the elders who stood before his father Solomon while he still lived, and he said, "How do you advice me to answer these people?" ...

And they spoke to him, saying, "If you will be a servant to these people today, and serve them, and answer them, and speak good words to them, then

they will be your servants forever."

But he rejected the advice which the elders had given him, and consulted the young men who had grown up with him.

These young men advised him to say to the people, **My little finger shall be thicker than my father's waist! And now, whereas my father put a heavy yoke on you, I will add to your yoke; my father chastised you with whips, but I will chastise you with scourges!' "**

So **The king answered the people roughly ... according to the advice of the young men... Now when all Israel saw that the king did not listen to them,** they made Jeroboam king over 10 tribes of Israel and Rehoboam was left ruling just 2 tribes. (1 Kings 12: 3-20)

XII

PUT IT IN WRITING

After you have passed through your impasses and agreed on a solution, draw up a formal agreement detailing who is to do what and by when and the consequences of failing to do so.

If you have been unable to pass through the impasses, move on to the next section of third party mediation.

C

THE THIRD CONFLICT

THIRD PARTY MEDIATION

THE THIRD CONFLICT

KING SOLOMON

& THE TWO WOMEN

Now two women who were harlots came to the king, and stood before him. And one woman said, "O my lord, this woman and I dwell in the same house; and I gave birth while she was in the house. Then it happened, the third day after I had given birth, that this woman also gave birth. And we were together; and no one was with us in the house, except the two of us in the house.

And this woman's son died in the night, because she lay on him. So she arose in the middle of the night and took my son from my side, while your maidservant slept, and laid him in her bosom, and laid her dead child in my bosom.

And when I rose in the morning to nurse my son, there he was, dead. But when I had examined him in the morning, indeed, he was not my son whom I had borne."

Then the other woman said, "No! But the living one is my son, and the dead one is your son." And the first woman said, "No! But the dead one is your son, and the living one is my son."

Thus they spoke before the king. And the king said, "The one says, 'This is my son, who lives, and your son is the dead one'; and the other says, 'No! But your son is the dead one, and my son is the living one.' "

Then the king said, "Bring me a sword." So they brought a sword before the king. And the king said, "Divide the living child in two, and give half to one, and half to the other."

Then the woman whose son was living spoke to the king, for she yearned with compassion for her son; and she said, "O my lord, give her the living child, and by no means kill him!" But the other said, "Let him be neither mine nor yours, but divide him."

So the king answered and said, "Give the first woman the living child, and by no means kill him; she is his mother."

(1 Kings 3:16-27)

THIRD

PARTY MEDIATION

Set The Time

Select A Private Place

Stockpile The Resources

Start With Introductions

Say A Prayer

Set The Ground Rules

Select The Priorities

State The Problem

Suggest Possible Solutions

Select The Ideal Solution

Step Through Impasses

Set It On Paper

When asked to mediate a conflict, before accepting the privilege, ensure you aren't affected by its outcome so that you don't put yourself in a compromising situation.

Then prime yourself spiritually and mentally for **The preparations of the heart belong to man, but the answer of the tongue is from the Lord.** (Proverbs 16:1)

Examine yourself to ensure the issues you are mediating do not afflict you. **First remove the plank from your own eye, and then you will see clearly to remove the speck from your brother's eye.** (Matthew 7:5)

Pray for Godly wisdom for **The wisdom that is from above is first pure, then peaceable, gentle, willing to yield, full of mercy and good fruits, without partiality and without hypocrisy.** (James 3:17)

You can pray King Solomon's prayer: **Give to Your servant an understanding heart to judge Your people, that I may discern between good and evil.** (1 Kings 3:9)

After introspection, commit to being impartial. Do not take sides regardless of what you think about the parties and their points of view.

Remain nonaligned because the success of the conflict resolution process depends on the conflicting parties respecting your opinions as unbiased and objective.

Learn from Jesus in the 1st conflict. He was nonjudgmental and neutral for He did not say whether the Pharisees were right or the woman was wrong. Then believe that you can do it and proceed with the following 12 steps.

I

SET THE TIME

Agree with all the involved parties when you will meet to resolve the conflict. Pick a time that is convenient to all so that they can all be available for the entire length of time that they agree to set aside for the negotiations.

II

SELECT A PRIVATE PLACE

Agree with the parties on a safe, neutral and private place to talk which should be free from interruptions and distractions.

Concur on an equal number of delegates for each party to bring to the discussions to ensure there is adequate room.

As you book the venue, request for a round discussion table as it is preferable to a square one. Ask also for similar seats especially if one party has more political power or monetary muscle than the others.

Then decide on the seating arrangement ensuring the mediator's seat is neutrally placed either in the middle or in front of the parties at odds like King Solomon for the 2 women **stood before him.**

III

STOCKPILE THE RESOURCES

Buy writing pads, pens, drinking water, cups, a whiteboard with markers (or a blackboard and chalk) and any other items that will support the conflict resolution process.

Ask the parties to bring their exhibits or evidence like the child whose parentage was being contested in King Solomon's case for when **The king said, "Divide the living child in two,** the child was in the room and the real mother **yearned with compassion for her son,** and the King saw she was the true mother.

If after listening to an overview of the conflict you realize that you will need assistance from lawyers, doctors, accountants, interpreters or other experts, ask for an equal amount of money from each of the parties to engage the services of a neutral specialist. Each party can also independently retain the services of a specialist they trust.

IV

START WITH INTRODUCTIONS

Introduce yourself and your role first.

Then present the parties to each other stating their relationships e.g. spouses, personal lawyers or business partners.

Don't skip this step as all should know those present and privy to their problems. If you don't know them well, let them introduce themselves like in Solomon's case for **One woman said, "O my lord, this woman and I dwelling the same house.**

V

SAY A PRAYER

Put the parties in a peaceful mode for negotiating by praying to the **Lord of hosts, who is wonderful in counsel and excellent in guidance.** (Isaiah 28:29)

Ask that you may be filled with the knowledge of His will in all wisdom and spiritual understanding. (Colossians 1:9) This will enable you to resolve the conflict speedily and amicably.

VI

SET THE GROUND RULES

For the talks to proceed civilly, read them the following rules and **Let all things be done decently and in order.** (I Corinthians 14:40)

THOU SHALL

KEEP THE DISCUSSIONS CONFIDENTIAL

Debate your case with your neighbor,

and do not disclose the secret to another. (Proverbs 25:9)

THOU SHALL

KEEP THE DISCUSSIONS TRUTHFUL

You shall not bear false witness against your neighbor. (Deuteronomy 5:20)

A false witness will not go unpunished, and he who speaks lies will not escape. (Proverbs 19:5)

THOU SHALL NOT

INTERRUPT SPEAKERS

You shall wait in silence until the person speaking finishes speaking and then look to the mediator to give you permission to voice your views no matter how pressing your points may be.

THOU SHALL NOT

USE FOUL LANGUAGE

Cursing, insults, threats and all other forms of foul language are forbidden.

Let all bitterness, wrath, anger, clamor, and evil speaking be put away from you, with all malice. (Ephesians 4:31)

Remember that **Whoever says, "You fool!" shall be in danger of hell fire.** (Matthew 5:22) If, for example, a person feels that they were deceived they should say, *"Based on what they said, I felt that I was lied to"* and not call anyone a liar.

Then focus on the offensive words and actions and not on the person who uttered or executed them.

VII

SELECT THE PRIORITIES

If there are many contentious issues, let them choose the most pressing one that they will tackle at that meeting.

If there is no consensus, ask each party to list their 3 most important conflicts in order and then choose from their lists the most commonly mentioned issue and address it at that first meeting.

Urge them to focus on that one issue and leave the others for future meetings.

VIII

STATE THE PROBLEM

Give each party adequate time to speak and state their problem for **The first one to plead his cause seems right, until his neighbor comes and examines him.** (Proverbs 18:17)

Emulate Jesus for after the Pharisees had spoken, **Jesus stooped down and wrote on the ground with His finger.** (John 8:2-11) He may have done this to give the woman time to speak. Though she did not utilize her time, the opportunity was there. So give all parties a chance to present their problems.

King Solomon also let each woman express herself fully as all parties should feel that their input is vital for reaching a workable and livable solution.

If one person is taking too long to present their case, set an equal time limit such as 5 minutes for all parties. If several members of one party want to speak, ask them to designate a speaker.

If you sense one party is not clear on an issue, ask the other parties to clarify it or urge them to seek clarification for themselves. This will avoid the confusion caused by using vague terms or by the using same word but with different meanings to different groups of people.

IX

SUGGEST POSSIBLE SOLUTIONS

After all the parties have stated their problems, ask them to write down all the possible solutions to the conflict.

Advise them not to censor the probable solutions. Let them just brainstorm and list them down. You can request, for example, for 10 plausible solutions from each party.

X

SELECT THE IDEAL SOLUTION

After listing the possibilities, let them start evaluating each potential solution and pick the perfect one as a group.

Remind them that the ideal solution(s) should solve at least one problem for each party or meet some of the needs of all parties and not necessarily all the needs of all the parties (though this would be the better option). It should also adhere to Biblical principles and comply with the laws of the land

XI

STEP THROUGH IMPASSES

If the parties are unable to agree on a solution, adjourn the discussions.

Let them sit in silence or drink tea or other refreshments. They can even take a weekend break to regroup and discuss in privacy how best to proceed.

During the break consider changing the seating arrangements as it may give them a different feel when they return to the negotiations.

When they resume, ask them, *"What will happen if we don't resolve this conflict?"*

This question helps them refocus on why they must resolve it and not on why they can't resolve it as it reminds them of the stress stemming from the conflict and the consequences of not reaching a consensus such as legal fees and time spent in court.

Remind them of Proverbs 25:8-10: **Do not go hastily to court; for what will you do in the end, when your neighbor has put you to shame? Debate your case with your neighbor.**

Advice them therefore to compromise and choose their own solution for once the issue is in court, they will have to watch from the sidelines as the law takes its course and decides how the conflict will be resolved.

Then encourage them to adopt a win – win approach and work as allies to find a mutually acceptable solution for this strategy ensures that they emerge as co-winners through cooperation. It also changes tone of their conversation from one of cutthroat competition to that of collaboration compromise.

Urge them to also think outside the proverbial box for a solution like Jesus when He said, **"He who is without sin among you, let him throw a stone at her first."** (John 8:2-11)

As the mediator you can use your own wisdom like King Solomon to broker a solution for the parties for **The king said, "Divide the living child in two, and give half to one, and half to the other."**

Then the woman whose son was living ... yearned with compassion for her son; and she said, "O my lord, give her the living child, and by no means kill him!" But the other said, "Let him be neither mine nor yours, but divide him."

So the king answered and said, "Give the first woman the living child, and by no means kill him; she is his mother."

Present your proposals of possible solutions as options in neutral terms and not as imperial directives.

E.g. *"How about if party X takes custody of the living child for one month and then party Y has custody the next month?"*

E.g. *"How about if party X works full time for money to maintain the child while party Y stays at home to take care of the child?"*

E.g. *"How about if party X works mornings and takes care of the child in the afternoons while party Y does the reverse?"*

E.g. *"How about if you both work to pay for the child's upkeep and hire a nanny?"*

Offer to meet with them after a certain period to review how well or poorly the arrangement is working so that they don't feel trapped by it.

Daniel did this when there was a conflict of diet between him and their steward for he said to him, **Please test your servants for 10 days, and let them give us vegetables to eat and water to drink. Then let our appearance be examined before you ... so he consented with them in this matter, and tested them 10 days** (Daniel 1:12-14)

You can also help them pass through the deadlock by asking them questions.

E.g. *"Party X, what is the best and worst thing that would happen to your interests if you adopted the child?"*

E.g. *"Party X, what is the best and worst thing that would happen to your interests if you let party Y adopt the child?"*

E.g. *"Party X, what are you willing to give party Y so that they can let you adopt the child?"*

E.g. *"Party X, what would you want from party Y so that you can let them adopt the child?"*

Repeat the questioning format for all the parties using all the possible solutions.

You can also help them barter solutions to fill each other's needs by asking **E.g.**

Mediator: *"Party Y, what 3 things can you do to help Party X solve problem 1 of taking care of the living child's expenses in exchange of weekly visitation rights?"*

Party Y: *"I can do activity I, II, III*

Mediator: *"Party X, choose 2 of these of activities for Party Y to do for you."*

Mediator: *"Party X, what 3 things can you do to help Party Y solve problem 2 of burying the dead child in exchange of them moving out of your communal house?"*

Party X: *"I can do activity I, II, III*

Mediator: *"Party Y, choose 2 of these activities for Party X to do for you."*

Repeat these questions for all the parties to ensure that each party has at least one of their top needs met.

In addition, constantly remind them to redirect the discussion from the impasses to new areas which may offer solutions.

E.g. *"As a postmortem was not done, let us not focus on how the dead child died and whose child he was. Instead, consider splitting the cost of DNA tests to determine the living child's biological mother?"*

If they reach a moral dilemma in their discussions, use the **Sword of the spirit** which is **The word of God** (Ephesians 6:17) to point them in the right direction.

XII

SET IT ON PAPER

Once they concur, draw up an agreement detailing who will do what, where, when and the penalty for breaching it. Read it aloud to ascertain its accuracy and let them sign it to signify adopting it.

They can also perform symbolic actions like exchanging cheques, rings or sandals like Boaz did after they settled he'd marry Ruth for **This was the custom ... to confirm anything: one man took off his sandal and gave it to the other, and this was confirmation.** (Ruth 4:7)

D

THE AVERTED CONFLICT

CONFLICT REDUCTION AND PREVENTION

THE AVERTED CONFLICT

JESUS, MARY

& THE PHARISEE

One of the Pharisees asked Him to eat with him. And He went to the Pharisee's house, and sat down to eat.

And behold, a woman in the city who was a sinner, when she knew that Jesus sat at the table in the Pharisee's house, brought an alabaster flask of fragrant oil, and stood at His feet behind Him weeping; and she began to wash His feet with her tears, and wiped them with the hair of her head; and she kissed His feet and anointed them with the fragrant oil.

Now when the Pharisee who had invited Him saw this, he spoke to himself, saying, "This Man, if He were a prophet, would know who and what manner of woman this is who is touching Him, for she is a sinner."

And Jesus answered and said to him, "Simon, I have something to say to you." So he said, "Teacher, say it."

"There was a certain creditor who had two debtors. One owed 500 denarii, and the other 50. And when they had nothing with which to repay, he freely forgave them both. Tell Me, therefore, which of them will love him more?"

Simon answered and said, "I suppose the one whom he forgave more." And He said to him,

"You have rightly judged."

Then He turned to the woman and said to Simon, "Do you see this woman?

I entered your house; you gave Me no water for My feet, but she has washed My feet with her tears and wiped them with the hair of her head.

You gave Me no kiss, but this woman has not ceased to kiss My feet since the time I came in.

You did not anoint My head with oil, but this woman has anointed My feet with fragrant oil.

Therefore I say it you, her sins, which are many, are forgiven, for she loved much. But to whom little is forgiven, the same loves little."
(Luke 7:36-47)

CONFLICT REDUCTION AND PREVENTION

Do Not Start Conflicts

Do Respond Appropriately

Draw On Parables

Disagree Agreeably

Depend On Jesus Christ

Do The Word And Heed The Law

Do Mind Your Own Business

Discipline Yourself

Demarcate Your Boundaries

Depart From The Scoffer

Drop Offences After Forgiving

Define And Document The Rules

Since it is difficult for any organization to progress and prosper if its members are entangled in conflicts or spend most of their time resolving them;

And since it takes more energy to resolve a conflict that to prevent one for **A brother offended is harder to win than a strong city** (Proverbs 18:19);

And since **Contentions are like the bars of a castle** (Proverbs 18:19) which can stop you, your family or business from being aided by those you are conflicting with;

And since you don't know when you'll need their help in a crisis for **Better is a neighbor nearby than a brother faraway,** (Proverbs 27:10) use these 12 tactics to prevent conflicts and **Avoid foolish and ignorant disputes, knowing that they generate strife.**(2 Timothy 2:23)

I

DO NOT START CONFLICTS

Though publicly slighted, Jesus behaved graciously and didn't create a scene after **The Pharisee asked Him to eat with him. And He went to the Pharisee's house** but the Pharisee didn't anoint His head with oil or wash His feet as was the custom.

Copy Him and conduct yourself civilly when wronged for **It is honorable for a man to stop striving, since any fool can start a quarrel.** (Proverbs 20:3)

In addition, know that you don't have to fight every time you are provoked for **The discretion of a man makes him slow to anger, and his glory is to overlook a transgression. (Proverbs 19:11). So, Be swift to hear, slow to speak, slow to wrath.** (James 1:19) Ignore minor slurs and **Do not take to heart everything people say** (Ecclesiastes 7:21) or do.

Conversely, don't start conflicts like the Pharisees in the 1st conflict. **Do not strive with a man without cause, if he has done you no harm.** (Proverbs 3:30)

Do not also create conflicts between those living or working together harmoniously for **One who sows discord among brethren** (Proverbs 6:16-19) is among the 7 things that are an abomination to the Lord.

II

DO RESPOND APPROPRIATELY

In addition to not kissing or anointing Jesus, the Pharisee also thought negatively of Him when Mary, for **It was that Mary who anointed the Lord with fragrant oil and wiped His feet with her hair** (John 11:2), begun to wash His feet.

He spoke to himself, saying, "This Man, if He were a prophet, would know who and what manner of woman this is who is touching Him, for she is a sinner."

And Jesus answered and said to him, "Simon, I have something to say to you." So he said, "Teacher, say it." Then Jesus diplomatically taught him about the creditor who had forgiven his 2 debtors.

Though Jesus felt his public snub and saw his irreverent thoughts, He remained calm and chose the right moment and the right words so that He could respond constructively rather than just react counterproductively.

So, refuse to be drawn into fights and conflicts even when you have been provoked and re-provoked. Restrain yourself like Jesus and respond respectfully.

III

DRAW ON PARABLES

Emulate Jesus and use parables to avert conflicts. He told of **A certain creditor who had two debtors. One owed 500 denarii, and the other 50. And when they had nothing with which to repay, he freely forgave them both.**

By asking the Pharisee **Which of them will love him more?"** he helped him see why Mary, a well known sinner, and thus the forgiven 500 denarii debtor, would express her great love by washing His feet with her tears, drying them with her hair and anointing them with perfume.

The Pharisee on the other hand, who most likely considered himself the 50 denarii debtor in comparison to Mary's many know sins, hadn't even loved his invited guest enough to perform the customary host rites for as Jesus said, **To whom little is forgiven, the same loves little.**

In another incident, Jesus used a short story to evade a conflict for **He went into their synagogue. And behold, there was a man who had a withered hand. And they asked Him, saying, "Is it lawful to heal on the Sabbath?" – that they might accuse Him.**

Then He said to them, **"What man is there among you who has one sheep, and if it falls into a pit on the Sabbath, will not lay hold of it and lift it out?**

Of how much more value then is a man than a sheep?

Therefore it is lawful to do good on the Sabbath." Then He said to the man, "Stretch out your hand." And ... it was restored. (Matthew 12:10-13)

Jesus also used questions to avoid conflicts for It happened on one of those days, as He taught the people in the temple and preached the gospel, that the chief priests and the scribes, together with the elders, confronted Him and spoke to Him, saying,

"Tell us, by what authority are You doing these things? Or who is he who gave You this authority?"

But He answered and said to them, "I also will ask you one thing, and answer Me: The baptism of John – was it from heaven or from men?"

And they reasoned among themselves, saying, "If we say, 'From heaven,' He will say, 'Why then did you not believe him?' But if we say, 'From men,' all the people will stone us, for they are persuaded that John was a prophet." So they answered that they did not know where it was from.

And Jesus said to them, "Neither will I tell you by what authority I do these things." (Luke 20:1-8)

So learn from Him to think quickly and side step conflicts by using parables, proverbs, questions or even tasteful jokes.

IV

DISAGREE AGREEABLY

Learn to disagree agreeably, dispute charmingly, disapprove sympathetically, oppose pleasantly and complain nicely.

Jesus did so, for without creating strife, He let the Pharisee know his errors, for **He turned to the woman and said to Simon, 'Do you see this woman? I entered your house; you gave Me no water for My feet, but she has washed My feet with her tears ... You gave Me no kiss, but this woman has not ceased to kiss My feet ... You did not anoint My head with oil, but this woman has anointed My feet with fragrant oil.**

By tying Mary's actions to Simon's slights, Jesus complained tactfully and tastefully.

He also sensitively shifted His attention from Simon to Mary as He spoke to avoid unduly embarrassing him.

In addition, Jesus informed him in a nice way that He knew that Mary had made many mistakes for He said, **"I say it you, her sins, which are many, are forgiven."**

Therefore, understand that even when you have been offended, mistreated, judged or misjudged harshly, you can complain and defend yourself without generating discord.

V

DEPEND ON JESUS CHRIST

Jesus is saying to you, **Behold, I stand at the door and knock. If anyone hears My voice and opens the door, I will come in to him and dine with him, and he with Me.** (Revelation 3:20)

So open your heart's door today and invite him in as **the Pharisees asked Him to eat with him.** He will come into your life, teach you a new way of living.

Opening the door of your life for Jesus is very simple. All you have to do is to **Confess with your mouth the Lord Jesus and believe in your heart that God has raised Him from the dead, you will be saved. For with the heart one believes unto righteousness, and with the mouth confession is made unto salvation.** (Romans 10:9-10)

So pray out loud, "Lord Jesus Christ, You are the Son of God, come into my life and teach me a new way of living."

Then believe that after He died on the cross for our sins, God raised Him from the dead and we are now freely forgiven whether we had committed 50, 500, 5000, or 5,000,000 sins.

Let Him in and you'll avert conflicts for He says, **Learn from Me, for I am gentle and lowly in heart, and you will find rest for your souls.**
(Matthew 11:29)

Be humble and gentle in all your dealings for **A servant of the Lord must not quarrel but be gentle to all, able to teach, patient, in humility correcting those who are in opposition.** (2 Timothy 2:24-25)

Urge members of your home, ministry and business to treat each other courteously as this engenders friendship and reduces conflicts. If they do occur in this friendly environment, they are more likely be forgiven than if there was pre-existing animosity between the members.

Encourage them to **Be of one mind, having compassion for one anther; love as brothers, be tenderhearted, be courteous; not returning evil for evil or reviling for reviling, but on the contrary blessing.** (1 Peter 3:8-9)

VI

DO THE WORD & HEED THE LAW

Obey the 10 Commandments as set out in Exodus 20 and urge members of your home, ministry and business to do so too. Heed the first 4 to reduce your conflicts with God and improve your relationship with Him.

1. I am the Lord your God … you shall have no other gods before Me.

2. You shall not make for yourself … any likeness of anything that is in heaven … in the earth … in the water under the earth; you shall not bow down to them nor serve them.

3. You shall not take the name of the Lord your God in vain.

4. Remember the Sabbath day, to keep it holy.

Then obey the other 6 commandments to improve your interpersonal relationships.

5. Honor your father and your mother.

6. You shall not murder.

7. You shall not commit adultery.

8. You shall not steal.

9. You shall not bear false witness against your neighbor.

10. You shall not covet your neighbor's house … your neighbor's wife, nor his male servant, nor his female servant, nor his ox, nor his donkey, nor anything that is your neighbor's.

Learn from the woman in the 1st conflict who could have avoided her conflict if she had obeyed the 7th commandment.

Obey your country's laws also to avoid conflicts with the authorities. Comply like Jesus when the scribes **Sent spies ... that they might seize on His words, in order to deliver Him to the ... governor. Then they asked Him ... Is it lawful for us to pay taxes to Caesar or not?"**

But He perceived their craftiness, and said to them ... Show Me a denarius. Whose image and inscription does it have?"

They answered ... "Caesar's." And He said to them, "Render therefore to Caesar the things that are Caesar's and to God the things that are God's."(Luke 20:20-25)

VII

DO MIND YOUR OWN BUSINESS

Take good care of your family, ministry and business as you **Aspire to lead a quiet life, to mind your own business, and to work with your own hands.** (1 Thessalonians 4:11)

Be fair in your affairs for God, your children and associates are watching you. The latter two are also taking their cues from you. If you ration the truth, they will economize on it also resulting in more conflicts in your domains for **If a ruler pays attention to lies, all his servants become wicked.** (Proverbs 29:12)

Minding your business also includes minding yourself to ensure you are upright, wise, and advisable.

Learn from Nabal in the 2nd conflict who could have evaded it if he was upright and paid for David's protective services but **The man was harsh and evil in his doings.**

He thus acted foolishly in refusing to pay and his wife Abigail said **"This scoundrel Nabal ... Nabal is his name, and folly is with him!"**

He was also unadvisable for one man said **"He is such a scoundrel that one cannot speak to him."** So no one tried to reason with him and even Abigail **Did not tell her husband Nabal** when she went to meet David. (1 Samuel 25:2-38)

On the other hand, Abigail's reputation as **A woman of good understanding** egged that same man to tell her what had transpired between Nabal and David. She then acted wisely and sought David to resolve the conflict on behalf of her husband and saved their family, workers, and sheep rearing business.

So mind your own business, mind yourself and stay out of other people's affairs. Don't get involved or comment on issues that don't concern you and you will reduce the conflicts you are entangled in for **He who passes by and meddles in a quarrel not his own is like one who takes a dog by the ears.** (Proverbs 26:17)

VIII

DISCIPLINE YOURSELF

Whoever has no rule over his own spirit is like a city broken down, without walls. (Proverbs 25:28) So exercise self-control as it is superb self-defense.

Control your mouth for **A fool's lips enter into contention, and his mouth calls for blows** (Proverbs 18:6) as Nabal called for blows from David for **Nabal answered David's servants, and said, "Who is David, and who is the son of Jesse? ... Shall I then take my bread ... water ... and give it to men when I do not know where they are from?"**(1 Samuel 25:2-38)

Even if he wasn't going to pay David, he could have at least disagreed agreeably with his messengers and prevented this conflict by editing his words.

Therefore, let **He who would love life and see good days, let him refrain his tongue from evil, and his lips from speaking deceit. Let him turn away from evil and do good; let him seek peace and pursue it.** (1 Peter 3:10-11)

In addition, control your emotions and actions. Copy Jesus who did not explode after the Pharisee affronted Him proving that **A wrathful man stirs up strife, but he who is slow to anger allays contention.** (Proverbs 15:18) So, extinguish anger and kill pride for **He who is of a proud heart stirs up strife.** (Proverbs 28:25)

IX

DEMARCATE YOUR BOUNDARIES

Set clear personal boundaries so that people know when they are encroaching on your cash, space, time, affairs and property. Learn from the woman in the 3rd conflict who could have avoided it by locking her bedroom door. (1 Kings 3:16-27)

Let all affected parties know your stand on these issues and they will be less likely to step on your toes. If they do try to step on them, think quickly on your feet like Jesus and side step looming conflicts.

X

DEPART FROM THE SCOFFER

If it is possible, as much as depends on you, live peaceably with all men. (Romans 12:18) If it isn't possible, separate from the scoffer.

Abram separated from his nephew Lot to prevent conflicts for **Abram said to Lot, "Please let there be no strife between you and me, and between my herdsmen and your herdsmen; for we are brethren.**

Is not the whole land before you? Please separate from me. If you take the left, then I will go to the right; or, if you go to the right, then I will go to the left." …

And they separated from each other. Abram dwelt in the land of Canaan, and Lot dwelt in the cities of the plain. (Genesis 13: 8-12)

So, **Cast out the scoffer, and contention will leave; yes, strife and reproach will cease.** (Proverbs 22:10) **Note those who cause divisions and offenses, contrary to the doctrine which you learned, and avoid them.** (Romans 16:17)

Avoid foolish disputes, genealogies, contentions, and strivings about the law; for they are unprofitable and useless.

Reject a divisive man after the first and second admonition, knowing that such a person is warped and sinning, being self condemned. (Titus 3:9-11)

Note that this doesn't apply to marital conflicts for **To the married I command, yet not I but the Lord: A wife must not separate from her husband ... and a husband is not to divorce his wife.** (1 Corinthians 7:10-11)

X

DROP OFFENCES AFTER FORGIVING

After resolving your conflicts, forgive the other party, ask for their forgiveness and forget about the offense so that you can continue relating well with each other.

Emulate Joseph who forgave his brothers for selling him into slavery and disregarded the terrible deed for he said to them, **"Do not be afraid, for am I in the place of God? ... I will provide for you and your little ones. " And he comforted them and spoke kindly to them.** (Genesis 50:19-21) As a result, they were able to relate as a family once again.

So, forgive, disregard the offense and **Repay no one evil for evil.** (Romans 12:17) Even if the other parties' words and actions have hurt your feelings, tainted your reputation, messed your marriage, wounded your ministry or damaged your business, do not retaliate.

Learn from David and leave it to God and God did avenged him for **After about 10 days, that the Lord stuck Nabal, and he died.** (1 Samuel 25:2-38)

In addition, learn from the conflict, your mistakes and those of others to avoid repeating them for **Strike a scoffer, and the simple will become wary; rebuke one who has understanding, and he will discern knowledge.** (Proverbs 19:25)

XII

DEFINE AND DOCUMENT RULES

Clearly define the rules, regulations and codes of conduct as well as the acceptable and unacceptable behavior in your home, ministry or business so that each member knows what is expected of them.

These acceptable standards can range from suitable language, dress codes, punctuality to loudness of music and any other activity that affects other people.

Simplify the rules for example by making just 10 rules which cover the key areas of your family, ministry or business.

After defining the rules, document them like God who **Gave Moses two tablets of the Testimony, tablets of stone, written with the finger of God.** (Exodus 31:18) He wrote down the 10 commandments so that the Israelites would know what was expected of them.

Document the regulations and give each member their own copy or hang it in a communal place to prevent conflicts.

As the head of your family, let everyone know the general house rules for **Better is a dry morsel with quietness, than a house full of feasting with strife.** (Proverbs 17:1) In addition, write your will well in advance to prevent conflicts after you have passed on.

As the head of your ministry, write down what God has asked you to do through your ministry, the vision and its mission to reduce conflicts of interest both now and in the future when you will not able to lead your it so that others can continue moving forward without wasting time bickering.

In your business, put everything in writing. If it is a partnership, clearly lay down the distribution of responsibilities, profits and losses for each partner.

Let each concerned party know what is expected of them, when it is expected of them and what will happen to them if those expectations are not met.

ABOUT THE AUTHOR

Dr. Miriam Kinai is a medical doctor who received her Clinical Training in Mind Body Medicine from Harvard Medical School. She is also a trained Christian counselor.

You can visit her blog at
http://www.ChristianStressManagement.com

or follow her on twitter at
http://twitter.com/AlmasiHealth

Email enquiries to drkinai@yahoo.com with BOOKS as your subject.

OTHER BOOKS BY DR MIRIAM KINAI

SELF HELP SERIES

RESOLVING CONFLICTS JUST LIKE JESUS CHRIST

Resolving Conflicts just like Jesus Christ uses Biblical examples from Jesus Christ to King Solomon to teach Christian Conflict Resolution Strategies, Third Party Mediation Techniques, Conflict Reduction and Prevention so that you can increase the peace in your home, the productivity of your ministry, and the profitability of your business.

*****

CHRISTIAN ANGER MANAGEMENT

Christian Anger Management teaches Biblical anger management tips and self help strategies to help you manage anger instead of letting it manage you and destroy your testimony, life, family, and career.

*****

HOW TO OVERCOME SHYNESS

How to Overcome Shyness teaches you several practical things that you can do to break out of your cocoon of shyness the way a butterfly breaks out of its cocoon and does things that a cocooned caterpillar can only dream of.

*****

95

CHRISTIAN EMOTIONAL HEALING

This book teaches you how to heal your emotional wounds using Biblical principles and examples of people in the Bible who were hurt emotionally like Joseph.

✱ ✱ ✱ ✱ ✱

CHRISTIAN GOAL SETTING

Christian Goal Setting teaches you how to set and achieve your goals using Biblical principles.

✱ ✱ ✱ ✱ ✱

HOW TO ENSURE YOUR PRAYERS ARE ANSWERED

How to Ensure your Prayers are Answered teaches you the things that the Bible says hinder our prayers so that you can stop doing them and ensure that your unanswered prayers are answered. This book also teaches you several other things that the Bible says we should do to increase the chances of having our prayers answered.

✱ ✱ ✱ ✱ ✱

HOW TO ASSERT YOURSELF

How to Assert Yourself teaches you how to express yourself clearly to your superiors, peers, and juniors without being disrespectful or hurting their or minimizing what you want to say by using a simple assertiveness ASSERT mnemonic.

✱ ✱ ✱ ✱ ✱

HOW TO LOVE YOURSELF

How to Love Your Self teaches you several practical and powerful activities you can do to begin liking yourself so that you can eventually love yourself unconditionally.

❋ ❋ ❋ ❋ ❋

HOW TO STOP BEING A PEOPLE PLEASER

How To Stop Being a People Pleaser teaches you seven simple things you can do to stop being a doormat and cure the disease to please.

❋ ❋ ❋ ❋ ❋

CHRISTIAN SERMON SERIES

HOW TO SERVE THE BODY OF CHRIST

How to Serve the Body of Christ is a Christian Sermon based on the events chronicled in Luke 7:36-50, Matthew 26:6-13 and Mark 14:3-9 that teaches you how to minister to the Body of Christ today.

❋ ❋ ❋ ❋ ❋

CHRISTIAN SPIRITUAL WARFARE SERIES

These books teach you how to wage spiritual battles by using Bible verses as your spiritual warfare prayers, saying them as Christian affirmations, and using them in your Christian meditation sessions. These books include:

1. How to Fight Addiction with Bible Verses

2. How to Fight Condemnation with Bible Verses

3. How to Fight for your Faith with Bible Verses

4. How to Fight Weakness with Bible Verses

5. How to Fight for your Business with Bible Verses

6. How to Fight for your Country with Bible Verses

7. How to Fight for your Children with Bible Verses

8. How to Fight Infertility with Bible Verses

9. How to Fight for Your Marriage with Bible Verses

10. How to Fight being Single with Bible Verses

11. How to Fight for your Finances with Bible Verses

12. How to Fight for your Health with Bible Verses

13. How to Fight for your Job with Bible Verses

14. How to Fight for your Ministry with Bible Verses

15. How to Fight for Peace of Mind with Bible Verses

16. How to Fight for Self Esteem with Bible Verses

17. How to Fight Insomnia with Bible Verses

18. How to Fight Confusion with Bible Verses

19. How to Fight Danger with Bible Verses

20. How to Fight Death with Bible Verses

21. How to Fight Despair with Bible Verses

22. How to Fight Discouragement with Bible Verses

23. How to Fight Fear with Bible Verses

24. How to Fight a Foul Mouth with Bible Verses

25. How to Fight Impatience with Bible Verses

26. How to Fight Laziness with Bible Verses

27. How to Fight Loneliness with Bible Verses

28. How to Fight Temptation with Bible Verses

29. How to Fight Opposition with Bible Verses

30. How to Fight Lying with Bible Verses

31. How to Fight Poverty with Bible Verses

32. How to Fight Oppression with Bible Verses

33. How to Fight Pride with Bible Verses

34. How to Fight for Self Love with Bible Verses

35. How to Fight Worry with Bible Verses

36. How to Fight Sadness with Bible Verse

37. How to Fight Vengeance with Bible Verses

* * * * *

CHRISTIAN SPIRITUAL WARFARE

This is a compilation of the above 37 books on *How to Fight ... with Bible Verses* in 1 volume for easy portability.

* * * * *

CHRISTIAN AFFIRMATIONS

This is a collection of Bible verses that you can use to proclaim over yourself and your situation as you wage your Christian spiritual warfare because death and life are in the power of the tongue. (Proverbs 18:21)

✱ ✱ ✱ ✱ ✱

CHRISTIAN MEDITATIONS

This is a collection of awesome Bible verses that you can ponder as you wage your Christian spiritual warfare since out of the heart (or mind) flow the issues of your life. (Adapted Proverbs 4:23)

✱ ✱ ✱ ✱ ✱

CHRISTIAN SPIRITUAL WARFARE PRAYERS

Christian Spiritual Warfare Prayers is a compilation of awesome Bible verses that you can say as warfare prayers to make your prayers more powerful when fighting your spiritual battles.

✱ ✱ ✱ ✱ ✱

SWORD WORDS

This book teaches you how to fight spiritually with the SWORD of the Spirit which is the WORD of God. (Eph 6:17) It tells you how to wield your SWORD WORDS while wearing the armor of God and demystifies the enemy's devices. It explains the battle plan, how to position yourself and communicate with your backup.

✱ ✱ ✱ ✱ ✱

STRESS MANAGEMENT SERIES

MANAGING STRESS WITH THE WORD OF GOD

This book teaches you how to manage stress with Biblical principles, medically proven relaxation techniques and other stress relief activities. It helps you answer, " What is Stress?", "What is the Body's Stress Response?" and "What are the Symptoms of Stress?"

✳ ✳ ✳ ✳ ✳

RULES OF RELAXATION

This book teaches you 130 simple relaxation techniques from **A**ssert yourself, **B**reathe deeply, **C**ast your burdens, **D**rink herbal teas, **E**stablish social support, **F**ormulate realistic goals, **G**uard your heart, **H**ave complementary hobbies, **I**dentify personal stressors, **J**aunt, **K**eep the Sabbath, **L**isten to music, **M**editate on the Word, **N**ab a nap, **O**ptimize stress, **P**amper yourself, **Q**uash sin, **R**eason rationally, **S**chedule news fasts, **T**rust God, **U**se cognitive restructuring, **V**eto worry, **W**ork out, e**X**periment with aromatherapy, **Y**ield to God to **Z**ap job stress.

✳ ✳ ✳ ✳ ✳

MANAGING STRESS FOR TEENS

This book teaches teenagers Biblical principles, life skills and medical techniques to manage teenage stressors like addictive substances, sex, sin, peer pressure, emotions, bullies, their bodies as well as answer "Who am I?" and "Why am I here?"

✳ ✳ ✳ ✳ ✳

NATURAL BODY PRODUCTS SERIES

Books in the Natural Body Product Series teach you how to make skincare products as well as the benefits of various vegetable oils, essential oils, butters, and herbs to help you choose the best ingredients. These books contain recipes for normal, sensitive, mature, and dry skin as well as for managing cellulite, eczema, psoriasis, menopause, PMS, painful periods, arthritis, stress, sadness, mental fatigue, and insomnia. Books in this series include:

1. How to Make Handmade Natural Bath Bombs

2. How to Make Handmade Natural Bath Melts

3. How to Make Handmade Natural Bath Salts

4. How to Make Handmade Natural Bath Teas

5. How to Make Handmade Natural Body Butters

6. How to Make Handmade Natural Body Lotions

7. How to Make Handmade Natural Body Scrubs

8. How to Make Handmade Natural Healing Balms

9. How to Make Handmade Natural Herb Infused Oils

10. How to Make Handmade Natural Soap

11. How to Make Natural Skincare Products - this book is a compilation of the above 10 books on *How to Make* ... for easy portability. It teaches you how to make bath bombs, bath melts, bath salts, bath teas, body butters, body lotions, body scrubs, healing balms, herbs, and soaps.

* * * * *

AROMATHERAPY ESSENTIAL OILS GUIDE

Aromatherapy Essential Oils Guide teaches you the characteristics, health benefits, and uses of the following commonly used essential oils: Chamomile (Roman) essential oil, Clary sage essential oil, Eucalyptus essential oil, Geranium essential oil, Lavender essential oil, Lemon essential oil, Peppermint essential oil, Rosemary essential oil, Tea tree essential oil, Ylang ylang essential oil.

* * * * *

AROMATHERAPY CARRIER OILS GUIDE

Aromatherapy Carrier Oils Guide teaches you how to dilute aromatherapy essential oils with carrier or base oils and explains the characteristics and uses of the following commonly used carrier oils: Sweet almond oil, Sunflower oil, Olive oil, Jojoba, Evening primrose, Virgin Coconut, Fractionated Coconut, Apricot kernel, Avocado, and Rose hip oil.

* * * * *

HOW TO BLEND ESSENTIAL OILS

How to Blend Essential Oils teaches you how to mix aromatherapy oils so that you can create healing mixtures with pleasant scents.

These therapeutic blends can then be used to create healing massage oils, handmade lotions, homemade soap, candles and other natural products.

* * * * *

DARK SKIN DERMATOLOGY COLOR ATLAS

Dark Skin Dermatology Color Atlas is filled with clear explanations and color photos of skin, hair, and nail diseases affecting people with skin of color or Fitzpatrick skin types IV, V, and VI. Topics covered include Acne Vulgaris, Alopecia Areata, Anal Warts, Angioedema, Aphthous Ulcers, Atopic Dermatitis, Blastomycosis, Blister Beetle Dermatitis or Nairobi Fly Dermatitis, Cellulitis, Chronic Ulcers, Confetti Hypopigmentation, Cutaneous T Cell Lymphoma, Cutaneous Tuberculosis, Dermatitis Artefacta, Erythema Nodosum, Exfoliative Erythroderma, Gianotti Crosti Syndrome, Hand Dermatitis , Hemangioma, Herpes Zoster, Ichthyosis, Ingrown Toenails, Irritant Contact Dermatitis, Kaposi Sarcoma, Keloids, Keratoderma Blenorrhagica, Klippel Trenaunay Weber Syndrome, Leishmaniasis, Leprosy, Leukonychia, Lichen Nitidus, Lichen Planus, Lichenoid Drug Eruption, Linear Epidermal Nevus, Linear IgA Dermatosis (LAD), Lipodermatosclerosis, Lymphangioma Circumscriptum, Miliaria, Molluscum Contagiosum, Neurofibromatosis, Nickel Dermatitis, Onychomadesis, Onychomycosis, Palmoplantar Eccrine Hidradenitis, Papular Pruritic Eruption (PPE), Paronychia, Pellagra, Pemphigus Foliaceous, Pemphigus Vulgaris, Piebaldism, Pityriasis Rosea, Pityriasis Rubra Pilaris, Plantar Hyperkeratosis, Plantar Warts, Poikiloderma, Postinflammatory Hyperpigmentation and Hypopigmentation, Post Topical Steroids Hypopigmentation, Psoriasis, Pyogenic Granuloma or Lobular Capillary Hemangioma, Scabies, Seborrheic Dermatitis, Steven Johnson Syndrome (SJS) and Toxic Epidermal Necrolysis (TEN), Sunburn, Systemic Sclerosis, Tinea Capitis, Tinea Pedis, Tinea Versicolor, Traction Alopecia, Urticaria, Vasculitis, Vitiligo, and Xanthelasma.

✳ ✳ ✳ ✳ ✳